RESILIENCE

How to coach yourself into a thriving future

@WORK

amplify
an imprint of Amplify Publishing Group

SIMON T. BAILEY

"But somewhere deep in your psyche, there is a still, small voice that says,

'Wait!'

It's in that moment that our soul senses the divine timing of the universe."

— SIMON T. BAILEY

www.amplifypublishing.com

Resilience @ Work: How to Coach Yourself into a Thriving Future

@2024 Simon T. Bailey International. All rights reserved. This book is protected by the copyright laws of the United States of America. No part of this book may be reproduced in any form without written permission in advance from the publisher. International rights and foreign translations available only through negotiation with Simon T. Bailey International, Inc.

Second printing. This Amplify Publishing edition printed in 2024.

Inquiries regarding permission for use of the material contained in this book should be addressed to:

Simon T. Bailey International, Inc.
13506 Summerport Village Parkway, Suite 324
Windermere, FL 34786
407-970-1113
hello@simontbailey.com

Amplify Publishing Group
620 Herndon Parkway, Suite 220
Herndon, VA 20170
info@amplifypublishing.com

CPSIA Code: PRV0624B
ISBN: 978-1-63755-992-5
Library of Congress Control Number: 2023917868
Editorial Director: Dr. Larry Keefauver, www.doctorlarry.org
Copy Editor: Caroline Barthalomew
Proofreader: Kathleen Pothier, Positively Proofed, Plano, TX
Cover Design: Kendra Cagle, 5 Lakes Design, Wolcott, NY

Printed in the United States of America

DISCLAIMER:

The information in this book is not meant to replace the advice of a certified professional. Please consult a licensed adviser in matters relating to your personal and professional well-being, including your mental, emotional, and physical health, finances, business, legal matters, family planning, education, and spiritual practices. The views and opinions expressed throughout this book are those of the author.

Since we are critically thinking human beings, the views of this author are always subject to change or revision at any time. Please do not hold him or the publisher to them in perpetuity. Any references to past performance may not be indicative of future results. No warranties or guarantees are expressed or implied by the publisher.

If you choose to attempt any of the methods mentioned in this book, the author and publisher advise you to take full responsibility for your safety and to know your limits. The author and publisher are not liable for any damages or negative consequences from any treatment, action, application, or preparation to any person reading or following the information in this book.

The author and publisher make no representations as to accuracy, completeness, correctness, suitability, or validity of any information in the book, and neither the publisher nor the author shall be liable for any physical, psychological, emotional, financial, or commercial damages, including, but not limited to, special incidental, consequential, or other damages to the readers of this book.

Dedication

This book is dedicated to my children: Daniel, Madison, Ashley, and Chelsey. Also, and of course, to G-Pop's granddaughter Halo!

May the wisdom of this book allow you to peel back the layers of my heart and know what is inside.

I love all of you, and I believe in you.

Inspiration
FOR THE COVER

This cover was designed from a hand-painted canvas, created especially for this project. Throughout the cover artwork, there are circular paint strokes, almost like orbs, and then more fluid strokes in the center. The blue, purple, teal, and green "orbs" represent the main characters in the book. They subtly dance across the pages to represent who is having a conversation with whom, who is "in charge" in any given chapter, and they help tell the story in an abstract way.

On the cover, the colors are very saturated, but on the interior, the pages are predominantly white, with bits of this same paint treatment throughout. The orange at the bottom of the cover represents the campfire that the characters sit around, and the other muted interior colors and various painted elements serve to create visual interest and emotion for the reader.

— **KENDRA CAGLE,** Creative Designer

Table of Contents

Acknowledgements

I would personally like to thank all the mentors who have poured their wisdom into my life over the past 35 years. All of these individuals have painted their insights on the canvas of my mind through conversations, books, teachings, sermons, prophetic words, and by living with character:

Dr. Mark Chironna, the late Dr. Myles Munroe, the late Rev. Reginald Bailey (my Pops), Bishop Tudor Bismark, George Fraser, Les Brown, the late Keith Harrell, Willie Jolley, Joel Block, Randy Morrison, Dr. Nido Qubein, Jayne Warrilow, John Maxwell, Bishop T.D. Jakes, Bishop Charles Blake, Stuart Johnson, Merryl Brown, Dr. Denis Waitley, the late Zig Ziglar, and Frank and Theresa AuCoin.

I want to thank Dr. Larry Keefauver for being a literary Yoda in helping bring this book to life. Thank you, Caroline, for shaping this book into the finest one that I've written to date.

To the STBI team, Stevie Johns, you rock! Thank you for being Director of Business Development & Operations and making sure we impact one audience and one life at a time. You and our team are the best in the world.

Thank you to my family: my wife, Jodi, our children, and our granddaughter Halo. I love you dearly and thank God for all of you.

Foreword
— BY DENIS WAITLEY

Resilience is one of the essential skills individuals can possess in the post-modern era. Yes, people have problems, businesses experience setbacks, and society is witnessing a tsunami of transformation. Yet, somehow, resilient individuals like you find a way to bounce back stronger and better.

In this parable, *Resilience@Work: How to Coach Yourself Into a Thriving Future*, Simon introduces you to four characters: Hurry, Worry, Steady, and Ready, who meet at a weekly California surfing camp and over a campfire they divulge their work and life struggles.

Surfers learn to harness the tides of uncertainty and work with the breaking waves of unpredictability instead of against it. They embrace a mindset of persistent consistency. Like you, they learn to adapt the skill of resilience to accelerate into a new reality.

As you immerse yourself in their stories, you will discover the wisdom lying dormant in your soul's roiling ocean. Furthermore, uncover simple strategies that empower you to develop this crucial life skill that makes you a winner.

About Dr. Denis Waitley

Denis Waitley is a world-renowned speaker and author of 16 bestselling classics, including *Seeds of Greatness* and *The Power of Resilience.* His audio album, *The Psychology of Winning,* is the all-time bestselling program on self-mastery. Denis has worked with Olympic athletes, astronauts, and POWs, and he is in the SMEI speaker hall of fame. To learn more about Denis, visit **www.DenisWaitley.com**. Follow Denis on Facebook @ OfficialDenisWaitley

Introduction

BRILLIANT RESILIENCE

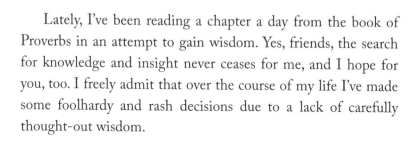

Lately, I've been reading a chapter a day from the book of Proverbs in an attempt to gain wisdom. Yes, friends, the search for knowledge and insight never ceases for me, and I hope for you, too. I freely admit that over the course of my life I've made some foolhardy and rash decisions due to a lack of carefully thought-out wisdom.

So, for many months, I pored over King Solomon's words. *(Most of the Proverbs are attributed to him, the ancient Israeli monarch, who was best known for his wealth, his wisdom, his writings, and his 700 wives.)* But, I realized during the course of this proverbial year that just reading and writing down quotes about wisdom won't get it, won't change me. I pondered what wisdom means to me, and then I thought, "Eureka!," wisdom alone isn't all of the answer. To have teeth, to be able to really matter, it has to be given away, shared, and it has to be applied to real-life situations.

Wisdom gained through experience is like a door that leads to the living room of life.

The quality we really need to thrive in our chaotic, fast-paced, competitive, confusing, ever-evolving world is wisdom paired with resilience, or more emphatically, Brilliant Resilience! Wisdom may be the glove, but resilience is the hand that goes into that glove. Resilience is the very application, the embodiment of wisdom. Wisdom is knowing what to do while resilience is actually doing it.

Why resilience?

According to the Gallup State of the Workplace report, roughly 7 out of 10 people are stressed out, dealing with high anxiety and borderline depression. The workplace imperative now is "well-being." Resilience decreases stress, reduces burnout, and increases psychological capital. Ultimately, resilient companies increase productivity, passion, and putting purpose before profit, thus becoming even more profitable.

Proverbs may not speak directly to resilience, but we can find it mentioned in other parts of the Bible:

- *"We are hard pressed on every side, but not crushed; perplexed, but not in despair."* **2 CORINTHIANS 4:8**

- *"Not only so, but we also glory in our sufferings because we know that suffering produces perseverance; perseverance, character; and character, hope."* **ROMANS 5:3-4**

- *"When you pass through the waters, I will be with you and when you pass through the rivers, they will not sweep over you. When you walk through fire, you will not be burned; the flames will not set you ablaze."* **ISAIAH 43:2**

Simply put, resilience is the capacity to endure and recover quickly from difficulties.

More profoundly, "Definitions have evolved over time but fundamentally resilience is understood as referring to positive adaptation, or the ability to maintain or regain mental health, despite experiencing adversity," according to Dr. Helen Herrman, et al., from positivepsychology.com.

On the same website, Laura Campbell-Sills states that, "Resilience is seen as more than simple recovery from insult, rather it can be defined as positive growth or adaptation following periods of homeostatic disruption."

And from a McKinsey & Company study: "But resilience is more than just the ability to recover quickly. In business, resilience means dealing with adversity and shocks, and continuously adapting for growth. Truly resilient organizations don't just bounce back better; they actually thrive in hostile environments... resilient companies not only outperform their peers through a downturn and recovery—they also accelerate into the new reality, leaving peers further behind."

This book, a parable if you will, is my endeavor to process what wisdom I've learned about the importance of resiliency— guidance I wish my younger self had known—and offer it to the world.

The book centers around a small group of professional people who meet at a weekly California surfing camp and become close friends while gathered around a campfire after each lesson.

The names of each of the main characters reveal their current situations:

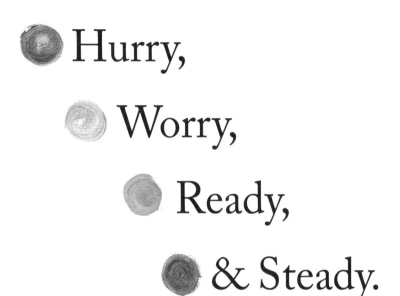

Hurry,

Worry,

Ready,

& Steady.

As *Hurry* and *Worry* divulge their work and life struggles, *Ready* and *Steady* share their own hard-earned wisdom and employ an exercise called the Friend-to-Friend Process. This process was developed by J. David Stone and Dr. Larry Keefauver, a licensed professional counselor, and is used in this story (with permission) to help Hurry and Worry recognize and work to change their dire situations. I have included the Friend-to-Friend Process because I believe it is an excellent way for people to tap into the inherent wisdom that is smoldering inside them. It is a way to resiliency.

Resilience@Work is autobiographical in that each of the characters represent some part of my own life's journey. That the story revolves around a surfing camp is no accident. I was in Cardiff-by-the-Sea, California, a few years ago and saw some people out surfing. When they came onto the beach near me, I asked them what the key to the sport was, and they said in unison, "It's the ability to pop back up." Boom, that hit me!

Surfing is the sport equivalent of resiliency. The very words surfers live by are the same words that resilient people choose: flexibility, spring, adaptability, buoyancy, persistence, doggedness, and tenaciousness. Surfers harness change rather than work against it. They must overcome constantly changing situations. They ride on top of the waves instead of being dragged down by them. Surfers must accelerate into a new reality and leave the past behind.

And that's exactly what resilience is.

I can't say it any better than this:

*"You can't stop the waves from coming,
but you can learn to surf."*

*(Quoted by Christine King in an online LinkedIn article titled
"People, Skills and Transformation" and attributed to another online
source, https://resilienceedge.com/the-resilience-edge/).*

What **Resilience@Work** is not is a quick fix, a silver bullet, or a magic pill. It is meant to be a guide to enhance and embellish your life at home, in your community, and at your place of business. It is meant to help you discover the wisdom that is lying dormant in the roiling ocean of your own soul and allow that wisdom to lead to Brilliant Resilience.

It is my ardent hope that this book will: invite you to find new waves of possibility as you surf into the future; flip on the light switch so you can see your story inside the main characters' stories; and examine the details of your work/life journey and not only imagine but also come to realize a brighter, better tomorrow.

And so, the story begins. In surfer speak:

"Yo, bros! I hope you're amped to read on. Prepare for some rad bombs and barrels coming your way! Cowabunga!"

Chapter 1

JUST IMAGINE...

Just imagine what would happen if you tried learning to surf by only watching YouTube videos. After completing the Surfing Zoom Video course, you'd go out and buy a board and launch into the high ocean surf. The next scene might well involve a drowning accident or more likely a heroic rescue by a lifeguard. Yes, despite having watched countless videos on how to surf successfully, you would no doubt be totally unprepared for the reality of huge, unpredictable waves that would surely wipe you out before you could even manage to get your footing.

As dangerous and unwise as learning to surf via video would be, how much more foolish it is to jump blindly and carelessly into the ocean of life—with all its storms, riptides, high winds, and strong currents—without the attentive coaching and mentoring of wise, experienced sages.

Our main characters, therefore, are not only on a mission to learn to confidently ride in the barrels and curves of monster waves and experience the joy of surfing, they are simultaneously—and perhaps unconsciously—trying hard to (or have already begun to) successfully negotiate the giant, often hazardous, and upsetting waves of life to find delight in their lives.

Okay, it's time to meet the players:

Hurry,

33 years old, lives in the fast lane.

He works hard, but for every step forward, he takes three steps backward, mainly because he doesn't pay attention to the details. Professionally, Hurry is constantly grabbing the next opportunity without vetting people or situations or assessing the risk/benefit factors. He has wasted countless hours and energy on "get rich quick" schemes that have nothing to do with his 9-to-5 job. Hurry wants to "hit it big." He thinks he has all the answers and rarely slows down to listen to others. His life is undisciplined, unstructured, and unplanned.

In his personal life, Hurry wants to date and eventually marry, but his impatience and know-it-all attitude have caused every one of his relationships to slip through his fingers like running water. Stingy to the core, Hurry would have to have "the jaws of life" to pry open his wallet, let alone his heart. He's always the taker… never the giver.

Pause for a moment and go to Appendix 1.

Take the self-test to see how much like *Hurry* you are.

Worry,

35 years of age, is drowning under waves of anxiety, believing that her work is meaningless.

Without hope, she gives up little by little each day as loneliness, a shrinking bank account, rising rent, and increasing debt threaten to wipe her out. She lives in a constant state of paranoia while waiting for the other shoe to drop. Worry has learned to cope by suppressing her thoughts and feelings when she senses she is around high-achievers.

Appearance is everything, she thinks. Worry puts on a façade that says everything is fine, but her soul bears a litany of past trauma from toxic work environments. She is overly concerned about the opinions of others, especially her boss. Worry has become so anxious that she finds it difficult to get through her workday and almost impossible to fall asleep at night. Worry feels the weight of the world on her shoulders.

Pause for a moment and go to Appendix 2.

Take the self-test to see how much like *Worry* you are.

Steady,

at 39 years old, has learned to embrace the currents of change and adapt accordingly.

Finding herself in a plum job at a major accounting firm, she realized she needed more meaning in her life. There were also issues from her past that she needed to deal with. So, after a life-changing sabbatical, Steady took the necessary steps to change her life. She transitioned out of her corporate job, and for the past 15 years has worked on becoming a freelance writer.

Steady invested in a writing coach, took online writing courses, attended writing retreats, and has reached a place of mastery in her natural gift.

Writing with the intent to help others find more meaning in their lives led Steady to take a six-month online course to become a certified life coach. Now, instead of chasing after work, opportunities flow to her like lily pads. She lives from a deep place of intellectual humility and is as calm and refreshing as an evening ocean breeze. She draws wisdom from a deep well of knowledge and understanding. She has found her voice and her freedom.

Steady enables her clients to move beyond negative feelings—shame, remorse, regret, and blame—caused by past failures and hurts. She asks probing questions and ably helps those she counsels to go beyond their surface issues and problems.

Ready

is 41 years of age. He literally found his voice and his passion at an early age, but he took several detours until he was able to circle back to that passion and then live it.

Ready's expertise is public speaking and writing, and he uses his oratorical and writing skills to coach and motivate others in their work and personal lives.

Ready has experienced divorce, a prostate cancer diagnosis, and contemplated suicide. But after a friend stepped in to help, and by working through regular therapy sessions, he has been able to turn his life around and live in a happy and healthy way.

Ready understands and applies the wisdom of Zig Ziglar, "If you help enough people get what they want, then enough people will help you get what you want." Ready is an influencer without a title. His core competency is connecting the dots and solving problems, with no strings attached. Honest and fair in all his dealings, Ready under promises and over delivers. He finds himself in high demand for speaking engagements all over the world and has authored several books.

As I pointed out at the beginning of the book, Hurry, Worry, Steady, and Ready met at a surfing camp in La Jolla, California. All four of them admittedly **"Barneys"** *(a surfing term for inexperienced, rookie, and rather untalented surfers)* and a bit **"clucked"** *(afraid of the waves),* they connected after the very first lesson. Three of them were very happy it was conducted entirely on the beach. Hurry, of course, complained that they weren't taking to the ocean right away!

After the lesson, the four were drawn to the *roaring* campfire...

...lit for those students who wanted to stick around and talk afterward.

Pleasantries were exchanged, compliments were shared, and a sort of weird bond was formed. They agreed to meet at the fire after the next week's lesson.

Lesson two over, Hurry, Worry, Steady, and Ready gathered again by the fire. Hurry was the first to speak, mentioning the fabulous trip he was going to take to Hawaii after surfing camp was over, after the big deal he'd been working on came through. Steady noticed that despite his confident words, Hurry was wound up, speaking too loudly and too quickly.

Worry was quiet for a while, thinking. Maybe it was the warmth of the fire, or maybe the fact that she thought she'd never see these people again after surfing camp was over, but she screwed up the courage to speak honestly.

> **Worry:** *You know, I had to scrimp and save, eat beans for several weeks, in order to afford to come to this camp. And now I'm afraid I've wasted that precious money. I'm not sure I'm coordinated enough to be able to surf. I'm not sure why I came.*

> **Steady:** *I bet you came because you wanted a challenge. You wanted to experience something thrilling, perhaps even to overcome some fear that is gripping you. I think you're looking for an adventure.*

Worry demurred, not sure if she should go further.

Steady spoke up: *We're all afraid, afraid of change, of the unknown, of that next big wave that just might topple us over. But, Worry, you're here, and that means you want to live life to the fullest. You want to not only ease but also conquer your fears. Am I right?*

Worry: *Well, yes, I guess so. Are you a counselor or something?*

Steady: *I'm actually a life coach. Besides writing, which is a huge passion of mine, my life's work is to encourage and motivate people to reach their goals.*

Worry: *Well, now I'm really glad I came! I could certainly use some life coaching.*

Steady: *I'm happy to help. Hurry, what brought you here besides getting ready for your Hawaiian vacation?*

Hurry knew in the back of his mind that his life at home was a juggling act that he was having trouble balancing. He also felt, for the first time in his life, that this was a safe environment and that he could open up without fear of judgment. He thought this was a chance-of-a-lifetime opportunity, not one that would make him a millionaire overnight, but one that could possibly alleviate his stress and allow him to live a calmer, longer, and more intentional life.

Hurry: *To tell the truth, I needed to get away. The stress is killing me. I am definitely on the treadmill of life, running hard but going nowhere fast. I want to feel important, so I boss my co-workers around and act like I have all the answers. In reality, I'm a mess. And that deal I was bragging about? I'm afraid it's another bust. I'm so tired of chasing the almighty dollar. Why can't I be content with what I've got?*

Steady: *I commend you for your honesty, Hurry! And I think you'll find that, here, you can free yourself of the distractions hounding you. You can live in the moment and surround yourself with things much bigger than yourself, like the majesty and beauty of the sea. You can make a new start, if you want. And I'd bet my life that we're all going to learn how to bounce back up onto our boards after getting knocked down more times than we'd like! We're going to learn to be resilient and courageous.*

Hurry: *I wouldn't mind that at all. It sounds like Worry and I did come to the right place, and we can certainly use some help and advice.*

Ready: *You know, Steady . . .*

...if you're familiar with the Friend-to-Friend Process, I think we could use it to help both Hurry and Worry.

Steady: *Exactly what I was thinking, Ready! It's getting late now, but why don't we start with it next week, if that's okay with you both.*

Hurry: *I'm on board. What about you, Worry?*

Worry: *I'm thinking it can only help.*

The four friends left the campfire a little lighter in their steps, looking forward to their lesson and the campfire next Wednesday.

Chapter 2

LIVING LIFE IN A *HURRY*

Back at surfing camp, the next lesson involved learning to paddle properly, one of the most demanding skills involved in learning to surf. Paddling, the students found out, takes a lot of brute strength and endurance, so the surfers were all pretty exhausted afterward. Physically worn out but mentally alive, the four fast friends headed for the campfire. Hurry and Worry were a bit suspicious about this Friend-to-Friend Process but happy to try anything that might jump-start a more confident and peaceful life for themselves.

Hurry: *I think we're ready to hear about this **Friend-to-Friend** thing you talked about last week. What is it exactly?*

Steady: *So, it involves asking three questions that hopefully will tap into the deep yearnings of your soul and then urge you to take the necessary actions to live them.*

Worry: *That sounds simple, ha-ha!*

Steady: *Seemingly simple, but deceptively complex.*

The three questions are:

What do you *want* for you?

What are you *feeling?*

What are you *doing* to get what you want?

These three questions address three levels of the human personality.

- The first question addresses our **thoughts** *(cognitive level)*.

- The second question addresses our **emotions** *(effect level)*.

- The third question addresses our **actions** *(behavioral level)*.

In the **Friend-to-Friend Process**, each question is meant to retrieve data from a person's different levels. And, obviously, no one has more data about you than you.

My purpose in asking you these questions is to act as a mirror by reflecting back to you the answers deep inside of you. I am not here to tell you what you should do. I am simply inviting you to uncover what is lying dormant in the ocean of your soul. You may wonder why I like using this approach. Well, I'll tell you…

Forcing solutions on you is worthless and disregards your capability to make realistic decisions about your life.

Insights

Everything a person needs to flourish is inside of them.

- Oftentimes, it takes inviting them into a safe conversation to identify the tools they already possess.

- Dr. Jean Watson, a nurse theorist and nursing professor known for her theory of human caring, said: "Many people do not fulfill their potential. They tend to look for solutions outside themselves. But the source of maturity, wisdom, reflection, insight, and mindfulness for developing an evolved consciousness is within."

Steady: *Shall we begin?*

Worry: *You first, Hurry!*

Hurry: *Let's do it!*

Steady: *Hurry, what do you want for you? By the way, I've heard answers like, "I want my husband or wife or boss or father, etc., to do such and such." This question isn't meant to be about others, it's only about you. We cannot change other people, just ourselves.*

Hurry: *I want my life to be meaningful and to matter.*

Steady: *What are you feeling?*

Hurry: *No one has ever asked me how I feel. I'm not sure. Can men really feel?*

Steady: *Funny, Hurry. But, yes, men can feel, and a lot more than just hungry and tired! Can you identify an emotion you're feeling?*

Hurry: *Hmmm… I feel sad, kind of overwhelmingly sad, to tell you the truth.*

Steady: *Thank you for your honesty, Hurry. May I ask what you are doing to get what you want?*

Hurry: *Not much. I guess I would say that I've been waiting for something to happen to me instead of making something happen for me.*

Steady: *Okay. Now I'm going to ask you the three questions again, but this time see if you can answer them differently.*

Insights

- A frequently asked question about the **Friend-to-Friend Process** is why it's necessary to keep asking the same three questions over and over. To an observer, it seems redundant and annoying, but to the friend who is struggling or hurting, getting to the answers is hard work and involves sorting important data from unimportant data. It may take some time for someone to contemplate and process his or her thoughts in order to answer on a deep level.

Be patient. Don't rush it.

Steady takes a deep breath, clears her throat, and then pauses for a moment. She leans slightly forward without invading Hurry's personal space, and then asks again: *What do you want for you?*

Hurry: *I want a plan for my life instead of flying by the seat of my pants. I want to feel peaceful and be in charge of my life. I want to get out of this rut.*

Steady: *Okay, what are you feeling right now?*

Hurry: *I'm feeling pretty discouraged and disappointed that I'm not further along in life. I've watched you and Ready over the past few weeks, and both of you are peaceful and calm. This makes me wonder if you ever have a bad day.*

Steady: *Believe me, there are still bad days, but I look at them now as challenges.*

Ready has been observing this back-and-forth dialogue.

He pipes up: *Hurry, may I ask you a question?*

Hurry: *No need to ask, go ahead.*

Ready: *What's the one thing you need to do right now to get what you want?*

Hurry: *I need to figure out my talent, skill, competency, or gift and then make a plan to find work in the area of my passion and expertise.*

Ready: *That sounds good, really good, but now I need for you to think about how you're going to get what you want.*

Hurry: *Well, that's the hard part, right? It's easy to talk about taking action but much more difficult to actually do. But, believe me, I'm ready and I'll come up with a plan of action this week. Thank you, Steady. Thank you, Ready.*

RESILIENCE @ WORK
Insights

- There is a book called *Your Natural Gifts* by Margaret Broadley, who was mentored by Johnson O'Connor, founder of Human Engineering Laboratory at Stevens Institute of Technology. In 1922, O'Connor worked for F.P. Cox, who started the General Electric Human Engineering Laboratory. Their first mission was to reduce overall costs by increasing the efficiency of their workers. O'Connor believed that everyone has an aptitude. In her book, Broadley wrote, "aptitudes know no economic or racial barriers. Nor does it matter if you're successful or unsuccessful, educated or uneducated."

O'Connor, Broadley wrote . . .

"believed that all human beings should have the opportunity to develop their natural abilities, their distinctive gifts, so they can attain fulfillment in their lives and through these gifts, contribute to society."

Steady, Ready, and Worry congratulated Hurry for his breakthrough, and as it was getting late, they agreed to head their separate ways.

Before leaving, though, Hurry asked if Ready would be willing to share his story next week after class. Without hesitation, Ready agreed.

RESILIENCE @ WORK FROM
History

The Scriptures remind us:

*"Everyone should be quick to listen, slow to speak
and slow to become angry."* (James 1:19)

*"A man's wisdom gives him patience; it is his glory
to overlook an offense."* (Proverbs 19:11)

*"The end of a thing is better than its beginning; The patient in spirit
is better than the proud in spirit."* (Ecclesiastes 7:8)

And from Marcus Aurelius, Roman emperor
from 161 to 180 CE,

"Perfection of character is this: to live each day as if it were your last, without frenzy, without apathy, without pretense."

Action Steps

- Hurrying through your work will lead to a multitude of careless errors. U.S. Founding Father Benjamin Franklin reminded us that . . .

"haste makes waste."

- Rushing to achieve your work goals can get you demoted or fired very quickly. Be diligent and mindful of details, and choose steady progress. Most projects are part of a marathon, not a sprint.

- Patience gives perspective and helps you correct errors or missteps along the way.

Insights

"Patience doesn't mean making a pact with the devil of denial, ignoring our emotions and aspirations. It means being wholeheartedly engaged in the process that's unfolding, rather than ripping open a budding flower or demanding a caterpillar hurry up and get that chrysalis stage over with."

— Sharon Salzberg, author

LEARNED FROM *Surfing*

- From online article "6 Profound Lessons That Surfing Teaches Us," by Lac Campbell, from The Surf Tribe: "Be patient and good things will come… As surfers, we're always waiting for something – the swell to pick up, the wind to swing, our friend to return the bar of wax he 'borrowed.' … By being patient, you give yourself the chance to enjoy the moments in between and you also increase your chances of getting what you're waiting for."

From San Diego Surfing School online article "5 Life Lessons Surfing Teaches":

"… finding balance when you surf is a constantly changing endeavor. Water can be a little unpredictable, as can the energy flowing through it, so even though you find the right balance to stand up, you can't rest on your accomplishment. You must continuously seek to retain that balance to see it through to the end."

- From another online article, "What Surfing Teaches You About Life," from Escape Haven (Sept. 25, 2017): "We all need patience, and surfing is one way to learn it over and over. You'll learn to wait for the right waves and be patient with yourself when you sometimes miss them!"

Chapter 3

READY AND WILLING

Thus far, the students had learned surfing etiquette and safety, wave dynamics, paddling skills, and board positioning and maneuvering, as well as pop-up moves (essentially explosive push-ups). Now it was time for them to master the proper riding techniques in the water. It was a perfect day with stable waves—also known as swells or "nugs" (not to be confused with another, somewhat illegal definition!)—continuously forming a good distance from the beach.

The four friends were excited and felt ready to take it to the water. Well, all except Worry, who thought she might have seen some "men in gray suits" (surfer talk for sharks) congregating out there. Hurry, Steady, and Ready urged her on, assured her they had her back, and got her out where the waves were breaking.

It was, shall we say, a rather humbling day for most of the students: several times up, only to wipeout time and time again. Sore and bedraggled, the four friends couldn't wait to plant their boards, peel off their wetsuits, and gather by the fire.

Other students noticed this weekly pattern and wondered about it. No one had a guitar and was singing Jimmy Buffett or Beach Boys tunes. No one was passing joints or "nugs" around. It appeared that the four huddled around the campfire were just talking. One student in particular asked Hurry what they talked about, and he replied that they were helping each other take charge of their lives and make necessary changes. Hurry explained the Friend-to-Friend Process and how it had jolted him into changing his life. The fellow surfer asked if he could sit with the group around the fire and just listen in. Hurry told him he could.

As promised last week, Ready was prepared to share his back story.

Ready: *Hurry, I can relate to you on so many levels. I, too, found myself in an unfulfilling job, a job that didn't make use of my particular talents. I'm lucky enough to have had the late Thomas J. Wininger, author of Your True DNA!, as a mentor. I was struggling to make sense of my life and mentioned it to him during a Zoom call. I'll never forget what he told me. He said, "You know you better than I know you. You only come to me to hear your answer. I am not qualified to tell you what to do. I invite you into a conversation to help you discover you."*

Hurry: *That sounds a lot like the Friend-to-Friend Process.*

Ready: *You're exactly right! One day Thomas asked me if I knew the difference between "qualified readiness" and "unqualified readiness." When I said no, he explained that qualified readiness is selective. It says, if this happens, then I will do that. For example, if I get the promotion I want, then I will totally commit my energy. In this approach, you're limiting what you have to offer until the right opportunity comes along.*

Ready continued: *On the other hand, Thomas told me, unqualified readiness is using your gifts and talents in every situation each moment of the day. It's knowing what you do best and asking the question, "How can I help you with what I do best?"*

It's living in the *moment* in order to make a future instead of waiting for the *future* to come to you.

Here's Ready's story about unqualified readiness.

From an early age, I realized that I had a gift for public speaking. When I was growing up in Buffalo, New York, my mother and father would have me give speeches in a storefront church that we attended. I would deliver these speeches on the trifecta days of Christianity – Easter, Mother's Day, and Christmas. I did this for years from the age of 5 to 14, and I loved it.

Recognizing my gift for public speaking, my mother enrolled me in oratorical contests that were sponsored by the American Legion, NAACP ACT-SO, and local organizations throughout the city. The more I engaged in these speaking events, the more my confidence grew, and more opportunities flowed my way.

I finished high school and went to college because society says you need to have a degree.

I started college and then dropped out. In fact, I dropped out of life for a while. Eventually, I went back to school, where I wasn't the best student. Truth be told, I was in the bottom half of the class that made the top half possible. Nevertheless, after attending three different colleges in 10 years, I finally finished my degree.

I found a job. It paid the bills, but I wasn't using my gift.

I was showing up every day, the lights were on in my head, but no one was home.

I had a guaranteed paycheck and benefits galore. I didn't want for anything and was on the fast track to a bright future career.

But, in the midst of living my own version of the American dream, something was missing. There was a hole in my soul, a gap in my mind, and a sense of being stuck in neutral and going nowhere fast. In fact, my name back then could have been Stuck or even Hopeless. One day, I reached a point where it just didn't click for me anymore. It had worked until it didn't, and I couldn't fake it anymore.

Professionally, I was content but not happy. I was successful on the outside but felt insignificant on the inside. I was going through the motions. I had settled for a chair, a check, and a cup of coffee in a cubicle farm. I woke up and wanted to be done, but I wasn't sure how.

Then, by happenstance or good old serendipity, I was invited to be the commencement speaker for the fall graduation at Florida A&M University in Tallahassee. On the phone with the person who asked me, I questioned her about the previous speaker. Turns out it was none other than U.S. Secretary of State Madeleine Albright! My mouth dropped open and, for a split second, I was at a loss for words. Then I was told what the honorarium amount would be. I blurted out that I would require twice that amount, while in the background my birdbrain was whispering, "What the heck are you doing? Have you lost your mind?"

I had no idea where this boldness, this chutzpah to ask for more, came from, but I held my peace. She told me she'd have to check with the president of the university and the finance department. Well, 48 hours later, she called back and said it was a go.

When I spoke at that commencement, there were 10,000 people in the audience.

During that speech, I found my spark again. I found my voice, my gift, my soul interest, the talent I had nurtured as a child.

It hit me then like a bolt of lightning:

My youthful orations were the little opportunities I took advantage of that could now lead me to work/life gratification. It was truly unqualified readiness in all its glory! This was confirmation for me that it was time to quit my job and pursue speaking and writing full time.

Insights

- Angela Duckworth, author of *Grit*, wrote: "Passion for your work is a little bit of discovery, followed by a lot of development, and then a lifetime of deepening."

- And Seth Godin, author of *The Practice*, wrote:

"Doing what you love is for amateurs, however, loving what you are doing is for professionals."

Hurry: *I am blown away. Thank you, Ready. As I reflect on the Friend-to-Friend Process, I now realize that the best hand to feed me is the one at the end of my own wrist. No one can do it for me. I must do the work.*

This past week, after our last fireside chat, I looked into the work done at the Johnson O'Connor Research Foundation and decided I'd take the aptitude test it administers. I've heard it's a great way to find out what career you're best suited for, one that will make use of my own unique talents and abilities.

Steady: *I'm so glad to hear that, Hurry! Do you mind if I pin you down and ask when you'll do it?*

Hurry: *I've got some time off coming up this month, so I plan to find the nearest location and register this week.*

Ready: *That's great news! Will you promise to let us know how it goes?*

Hurry chuckled, nodded, and stood up, along with the others. Worry gave Hurry a fist bump, and Steady and Ready asked if they could put their arms on his shoulders. Hurry nodded again. They looked him in the eyes, and said in unison . . .

"That's the Friend-to-Friend Process."

- From Benjamin Disraeli:

"The secret of success in life is for a man to be ready for his opportunity when it comes."

- "Luck is when an opportunity comes along and you're prepared for it." — Denzel Washington

- *"Be dressed in readiness, and keep your lamp lit."* (Luke 12:35)

- *"Tell the people: Purify yourselves in readiness for tomorrow."* (Numbers 11:18)

- *"Now therefore perform the doing of it: that as there was a readiness to will, so there may be a performance also out of that which ye have."* (2 Corinthians 8:11)

LEARNED FROM Surfing

From an online article from Dreamsea Surf Camp, titled "6 Life Lessons Learned From Surfing":

- **"You won't catch a wave by staring at it…** If you don't make an actual effort to catch the waves, they won't magically come to you… We can translate this truth to other aspects in life: it could be a job, or a relationship, or anything else you want to get in your life. … if you don't make any effort to get the opportunities you hope to 'ride' in life, they will pass underneath you or come down crashing hard."

- **"You won't be remembered for your wipeouts.** No you won't. When we enter the water we may feel like everyone is looking at us and judging every move we do, but the truth is that no one will come to us after surfing and remind us of that wave we lost or that time we fell… That's an important value we can take into our life. Sometimes we are afraid for what people will think about us and we don't take risks, but most of the time we are completely wrong. Go out there and try as many times as you can until you complete your goals!"

"**Celebrate every small victory.** Surfing is one of those sports that requires a lot of time and a lot, a loooot of effort. You cannot expect to be surfing like a pro in your first week, not even in your first year, but you can enjoy every part of the process, from standing up in your first whitewash to getting barreled or making an incredible maneuver. Same happens in life, blinded with the final result, we tend to ignore every small victory we make on our way to achieve something."

- "**Never give up…** Problems in life come in sets, like waves, but in between these sets there are always periods of calm that we can use to come back to our initial position or even go further. At the end, we have to keep paddling and keep fighting for what we want."

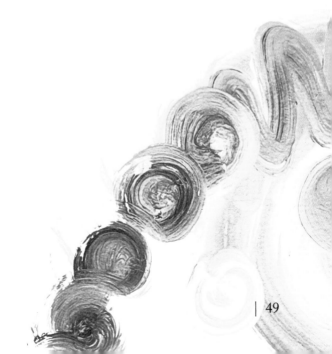

Chapter 4

OVERCOMING THE WAVES OF WORRY

The next Wednesday, offshore winds foretold another excellent afternoon for surfing. The four friends—Worry included—had what is called "surfer's froth": they were stoked and ready for the next level. Out beyond the lineup, or the takeoff zone, the instructors demonstrated cutbacks—changing direction by turning to go back toward the breaking and steepest part of the wave. A few at a time, the students paddled out to give it a try.

Again, it was hit or miss, pop-up then wipeout for most all of them. Still, exhilarated from the effort, Hurry, Worry, Steady, and Ready came out of the water, eager to gather by the fire.

Ready disappeared to his car and came back with an insulated thermal bag full of food—specifically tacos, lettuce wraps, avocado mash, and healthy vegetables. Steady provided the drinks—kombucha, coconut water, and cranberry, beet, and pomegranate juices.

Worry, who figured it was her turn to share her struggles, was glad for the diversion.

> **Worry:** *Boy, you two are serious about eating healthy, aren't you?*

> **Ready:** *Well, I don't know about you all, but when I get through with class, I'm famished. And as long as we're talking about healthy changes and self-discovery and accountability, I thought we should make it apply to our bodies, too.*

> **Steady:** *Right! Help yourselves!*

The student who had joined their group last week but kept to the outside of the circle walked up and asked if he could once again sit and listen. Everyone invited him in and offered him some food and drink.

Worry, emboldened by her courage in the water that day and by this new set of caring friends, took a deep breath.

Worry: *If it's okay with the rest of you, I'm ready to share my story.*

Steady, Ready, and Hurry nodded their assent.

Worry: *My dream since tenth grade was to be an engineer. I loved math and science in school, and I was always developing something in robotics class. My plan was to collaborate with my cousin, who also excelled in math and science, and start an industrial design and innovation firm.*

But after graduating from Gonzaga, I started to agonize over whether I had what it takes to succeed. No one in my family had ever done anything bold like start a business. I worried that my dream would land me in debt and disappointment, or worse, poverty and failure.

So here I am today, working in a toxic environment for a boss who piles more work on me than I can possibly get done.

I'm doing the job of three people and staying at it because I need to pay my rent and my mother's healthcare costs. I worry that I might be dying a slow death.

I work hard enough to keep my job and do just enough to keep from getting fired, but I heard through the grapevine that our company may be acquired by a larger entity. I'm worried that if that happens, my job will be eliminated.

I'd really like to date and meet someone I enjoy being with, but then I fret that if I do meet someone I like, he'd get to know me and decide I have too many issues to deal with. (At this point, Worry was crying.) Lately, I've found myself struggling to get out of bed.

Insights

- Authors Chris Crowley and Henry Lodge, in their book *Younger Next Year*, mention that scientists hypothesize how we replace about one percent of our brain cells each day. According to Dr. Barbara Fredrickson, a university professor, that's 1 percent today, another 1 percent tomorrow, amounting to roughly 30% by next month, and 100% by next season. So, every three months you get a whole new you, which is amazing, but stress and worry counteract this rejuvenation.

Scientists concur that worrying slows down the brain.

Ready put his arm around Worry and asked her to take three deep breaths.

Ready: *Worry, what do you want for yourself?*

Worry: *I want peace of mind.*

Ready: *What are you feeling?*

Worry: *I feel as if disappointment, discouragement, and despair are what I deserve.*

Ready: *What are you going to do about it?*

Worry: *I haven't the faintest idea where to start or what to do.*

Ready: *Any ideas swirling around in your head?*

Worry: *I suppose I could start each day with a positive expectation?*

Ready: *Great! How?*

Worry: *I guess I could identify what I am most grateful for.*

Ready: *What are you most grateful for right now?*

Worry: *Well, I'm grateful for being able to open my eyes and see the sun's rays piercing through my window.*

Ready: *How do you feel as you reflect on being grateful?*

Worry: *Hopeful, I think… maybe not so hopeless.*

Ready: *What else can you do to start your day in a positive way?*

Worry: *I really need to flip my negative thoughts into positive ones before they derail my day. I often find that I self-sabotage by thinking something will go wrong before anything even happens. I see now that I have been starting my days at a huge emotional deficit, and those tides of disaster just keep on rolling in.*

Ready: *How will you stay positive and keep an upbeat energy going throughout your day?*

Worry: *I could commit to taking small steps every day to bolster my self-confidence and gain some control over my life.*

Ready: *Anything else you can do to put yourself on the path to getting what you want?*

Worry: *I could talk to my boss about my crushing workload and look for opportunities to get involved at a low level with an engineering firm. I could ask my college professors for recommendations and spread the word about engineering being my dream.*

Once again, the conversation was another campfire chronicle. Hurry and Steady, along with Ready, stood up and moved to shake hands with and embrace Worry, who felt seen, heard, valued, and understood for the first time in a very long time.

The surfer who had joined the group realized that the weekly fireside chat was nearing an end. He introduced himself as Curious.

Curious: *Thank you for allowing me to eavesdrop. I've learned so much about myself while listening in. May I come back next week?*

Ready: *Of course! Steady, I'm thinking it would be interesting for the rest of us if you'd be willing to share your story next week.*

Steady nodded, and
the four *(now five)*
friends said goodnight.

Insights

- **You're responsible for creating your boundaries.**

  Here's a reality check: Boundaries are created—they don't come baked into your relationships. If you're constantly finding yourself in uncomfortable situations with people who want you to give more and more of yourself, it's likely because you aren't taking responsibility for creating boundaries.

- **You're not responsible for anyone else's reaction.**

  Oftentimes, people say "yes" for fear of disappointing or hurting someone else. Sound familiar? This fear often comes from an intense desire to be liked, and it's incredibly damaging when you lead with it in the workplace. This is partly because you're focusing too much on keeping others happy and not enough on achieving results.

- **Successful people know how to say "no."**

  This is something they've had to teach themselves because they, too, struggled with the "no" word at some point in time. But with science showing us that saying "no" improves productivity and mental health, none of us can afford to keep saying "yes."

In the words of business magnate Warren Buffett . . .

"The difference between successful people and very successful people is that very successful people say no to almost everything."

History

Solomon, the biblical King, was known, among other things (as I mentioned earlier), for his wisdom. According to 1 Kings, after Solomon made a sacrifice to God, God appeared in the king's dream asking what he would like to be blessed, or rewarded, with. Solomon asked for wisdom to better guide his people.

Here are a few of his wise words, which are still relevant today.

- "Worry weighs us down; a cheerful word picks up."

- "A sound mind makes for a robust body, but runaway emotions corrode the bones."

- "A cheerful disposition is good for health; gloom and doom leave you bone-tired."

Action Steps

- Choose to focus your thoughts, words, and feelings in the direction of your future instead of staying stuck in your current circumstance. Living in the past is often depressing and can produce anxiety. Focus on living your best present.

Maximize the moment while setting reasonable, attainable goals for the future.

- Never let negative emotions distract you from reaching your goals.

LEARNED FROM *Surfing*

From online article "6 Profound Lessons Surfing Can Teach Us About Life" by Lac Campbell, from The Surf Tribe:

- "Worry about only what you can control…Worrying about things you can't control will only lead to more stress and anxiety, so it's important to let these go and focus on the two things always within your control: your attitude and your effort."

From online article "What Surfing Teaches You About Life" from Escape Haven (Sept. 25, 2017):

- "**Believe in yourself**—… Ultimately what you believe you can do, you will do."

- "**Courage**—… is not about NOT being scared, but feeling your feelings and doing it anyway!"

- "**Adaptability**—Surf conditions are constantly changing and every set of waves is different… Being flexible and finding your flow is so important both in and out of the water."

- "**Mindfulness**—Surfing is an incredible practice of active meditation—if you are not practicing mindfulness, you'll fall off the board… You'll find yourself releasing the stress of everyday life and remembering what's important to you by truly embracing the moment. Learning the art of living in the here and now will bring happiness and so much freedom to all aspects of your life."

- "**Resilience**—… surfing will give you a master class on this. There are going to be times when you feel disheartened, but you'll learn to pick yourself up and try again. The more times you get back on the board, the stronger your resilience muscle will grow."

And from an online article from the San Diego Surfing School:

- "… **Floating Along May Lead to Nowhere**—You can sit on a surfboard all day and not get anywhere. Up and down to and fro as the waves pass under barely moving you. It's a good metaphor for life. If you just go along, never taking action, things will happen around you,… but you'll stay on that road to nowhere."

- **"So Seize Your Opportunities**—… the only wave a surfer ever regrets, is the one they let pass by them. Life is very similar. Most people tend to regret the things they didn't do, the chances they didn't seize, more than anything they did."

- **"And Lean Into Life**—… Surfing is the pinnacle of understanding your environment, working with it, working with your own body and, ultimately, leaning into it… You can't just stand there, or the power of the wave will knock you right over. Once you jump into life, you have to lean into it."

"Each day is God's gift to you. What you do with it is your gift to Him."

—T.D. Jakes, *Maximize the Moment: God's Action Plan for Your Life*

Chapter 5

MESSAGE IN A BOTTLE

This Wednesday was the last day of surfing camp. All of the students were anxious to experience the thrill of riding the big ones, to feel that indescribable joy their instructors kept talking about. Sure enough, cheered on by each other, the friends paddled out to the waves, separated, waited patiently, popped up at the right moments, made their drops and rode inside the barrels for the rest of the afternoon. Even Curious—who usually held back and observed—got into the flow.

Out of breath, but totally invigorated, they stumbled onto the beach, lay quiet for a bit, then began to laugh.

Ready: *Super day, right guys?*

Hurry (with a newfound confidence): *Shouldn't we say "akaw"?* (That's surfer speak for "awesome" or "epic.")

Worry: *Yes! Hey, that bottom turn was sick, no?*
More laughter, then the original group of four headed to the campfire, joined by Curious. This time, everyone contributed to the healthy fare.

Curious: *I can't wait to hear your story, Steady.*

A few silent moments passed as Steady finished her food then wiped her hands and mouth.

Here's Steady's story.

Okay, here we go… I suppose I should start at the beginning. I was born in Cape Town, South Africa, and my parents divorced when I was 14. My mom decided to relocate to London to be with her sister and brother-in-law, who had invited us to live with them and begin a new life.

After we moved, I never heard from my dad again. My name at that time wasn't Steady. It was Angry, Confused, Regretful, take your pick.

My mother found a job at a bookstore, and after several years, the owners decided to move to the English countryside and offered her the opportunity to buy the store. I watched as my mom made it work, despite the world shifting to digital books, trying innovative ideas so customers would come, browse, and buy. She is my hero.

After graduating from King's College and majoring in classical studies and comparative literature, I started my career at one of the Big Four accounting firms. I'm convinced they hired me because I could write and communicate well and possessed several of the soft skills that make an employee a good one. Skills such as listening well, empathy, and the ability to encourage and coach others.

RESILIENCE @ WORK
Insights

Valerie Strauss, education writer for *The Washington Post,* said . . .

"Broad learning skills are the key to long-term, satisfying, productive careers.

What helps you thrive in a changing world isn't rocket science. It may just well be social science, and, yes, even the humanities and the arts that contribute to making you not just workforce ready but world ready."

Steady continued:

After receiving several promotions and landing in the role of chief communications officer reporting directly to the CEO, I was making good money and traveling all over the world. Still, I wanted more or, more correctly, I needed my job to reflect meaning and purpose. I didn't really feel that my talents were being used in the best way. And I wanted a personal life. I didn't date because I was married to the job.

I decided to see a therapist and was introduced to the Friend-to-Friend Process. She asked me what it was I wanted for myself. I told her I wanted peace. I wanted off the treadmill, and I wanted to forgive my father for divorcing my mother.

She asked me how I felt, and I responded that I was mentally exhausted, emotionally depleted, spiritually empty, and personally unfulfilled.

She asked what steps I was going to take to get what I wanted. I told her that I'd been thinking for a while that I needed to take a sabbatical. I'd saved enough money to cover it and my boss had agreed I could take the time off. Everything was in place, I told her. All I needed to do was pick a destination and make the arrangements. The therapist asked what I hoped to accomplish on sabbatical.

I told her I wanted to find the 2.0 version of me, the next chapter of my life. She recommended I read the book *Halftime* by Bob Buford, which is about the author re-discovering himself and his purpose in life after selling his business. It was just what I needed at the time, and I'd highly recommend reading it.

I decided to rent a quaint studio near La Jolla Cove. The first few days were difficult since I didn't know how to unplug, unwind, or declutter my mind. But daily walks on the beach helped me find a measure of peace and calm.

One early morning on one of my walks, I saw an elderly man combing the beach with a metal detector. I approached him, and we struck up a conversation. He told me his name was Seeker, and that after having served in the military and then honorably discharged, he decided he'd spend what remained of his life searching for lost treasures. His wife had died, and his extended family members stayed away, embarrassed by his eccentric ways.

He told me about the day he'd dug up a weathered bottle that clearly had a note inside. Back in his garage, he'd freed the cork from the bottle and fished out the piece of paper, on which was written ...

Call unto me and I will show you great and incomprehensible things you do not know.

He said he was immediately floored, speechless, and humbled. These were the exact words his mother spoke just before she died. It had been her favorite Bible verse.

This find, this message from the past or from above, reminded him that he wasn't alone in his loneliness, that he may have been forsaken but he wasn't forgotten. He told me that at that very moment he got down on his knees and asked God to come into his life and help him find the everlasting and eternal treasure in Him.

Since that day, Seeker has found significance by starting and now running a ministry for the homeless. That's how he serves God.

Worry: *How did that encounter change you, Steady?*

Steady: *I started praying to God. I had always believed in Him, but I hadn't made room for Him in my busy life. I began journaling and assessing my gifts, skills, and competencies. I realized that the part of my work I enjoyed the most was advising my co-workers, inviting them into meaningful conversations, inadvertently helping them make discoveries about themselves.*

I decided to create an exit strategy. I've always loved to write, so I enrolled in an online writing course. I eliminated all debt and made a date with destiny. The following year, my birthday present to myself was to walk away from what I had—a paycheck and an important job—to what I could become—a presence-driven leader who was led by divine destiny. In the words of author Pat Morley, I found my "second wind for the second half."

I absolutely love my work now as an adviser to corporations helping CEOs train, motivate, and retain their employees. One of my clients told me my name should be Steady, and I try to live up to that every day.

Curious, Worry, Hurry, and Ready were silent for a few minutes, each processing Steady's story and watching intently as the embers died down and the evening air became chilly.

It was Worry who broke the silence.

Worry: *I know this transformative and healing time has to end with our surfing lessons, but I don't want our deep friendship to end with it. I'd love it if we all shared our information and at least got together on Zoom or through group emails.*

Hurry: *You read my mind, Worry!*

Steady, Ready and Curious, too, energetically agreed, and right there by the fire, they shared their information, gave each other hugs, and promised to stay in touch.

- From Marcus Aurelius: "Be like the cliff against which the waves continually break; but it stands firm and tames the fury of the water around it."

- 2 Peter 1:6-7: "And knowledge with self-control, and self-control with steadfastness, and steadfastness with godliness, and godliness with brotherly affection, and brotherly affection with love."

- "Lord, give me firmness without hardness, steadfastness without dogmatism, love without weakness." — Jim Elliot

- And from Victor Hugo:

"Change your opinions, keep to your principles; change your leaves, keep intact your roots."

LEARNED FROM Surfing

From Surf Tribe's online article "6 Profound Lessons That Surfing Can Teach Us About Life":

- **"Respect is a two-way street**—Respect in surfing is a big deal. It brings order to a chaotic lineup and a sense of appreciation for the environment. But respect is a two-way street – we must show it to get it. By respecting others and being humble, we create an environment in which we can all surf together peacefully. And by respecting the waves, beaches and surf breaks, we ensure that future generations will be able to enjoy them too."

- **"Nature is to be treasured**—If you ever want proof that Mother Nature is a powerful force, try surfing big waves. However, if you also want proof that she's to be looked after and respected, try surfing in a place where there's very little of her left. Nature is both mighty and fragile at the same time."

- **"Life is full of highs and lows** – Life is kind of like a wave in the sense that there are both peaks and dips. Sometimes you feel like an absolute rockstar. Other times you feel like the human equivalent of a discarded soft top surfboard. Just remember that you can't stop the waves but you can learn to surf, which is to say that while the bad times will inevitably come, we have faith that you can always ride them out."

"In a world of constant flux, those who are steady are not easily shaken or moved by tides of despair."

Epilogue

One of the most powerful words in the English language is "serendipity," the phenomenon of finding valuable and positive things not intentionally sought after.

Hurry, Worry, Steady, Ready, and Curious came to the same camp to learn to surf and, as serendipity would have it, were drawn to each other. Without them even realizing it, the lessons they grasped by learning to surf became a part of them, and because their earnest fireside talks deepened and personalized these lessons, they were forever changed.

I'm going to end the story in an upbeat way—because I wrote it and I can—

by telling you that the five friends stayed in touch through the years. Aware of the potency of the **Friend-to-Friend Process** to effect change, they each found ways to use it to help struggling co-workers, friends, family members, and acquaintances.

They became foxhole friends, holding each other accountable for their decisions and encouraging each other through good times and bad. They showed up for the big events in each other's lives and even met back in California for a few surfing trips. Hurry, Worry, and Curious outgrew their names, each having found meaningful, soul-satisfying work. Worry said she was ready to be Content. Hurry changed his name to Diligent. Curious became Fearless. And they all embraced Brilliant Resiliency because they had learned that's the way to surf, and it's also the surest way to live and work productively and contentedly in this world.

Insights

- *Brilliant Resilience* understands that every shift, setback, or success produces a belief that, yes, you can overcome it, and, yes, you will come out stronger and better for it.

- *Brilliant Resilience* is discovering that when you bounce back you are able to do so because, in the midst of uncertainty, you have invested your energy in finding the solution instead of wallowing in the problem.

- *Brilliant Resilience* is reframing change as your friend, not your foe, and seeing change as a brilliant opportunity.

- *Brilliant Resilience* is shifting from a 5-by-7 limited reality to frameless, unlimited possibility.

- *Brilliant Resilience* allows you to gather the winds of uncertainty, rise above the clouds of disappointment, and push through hurricanes of failure by mastering the courage to say: *I will make it. I will thrive.*

- *Brilliant Resilience* is moving past the past. Resilient people have the ability to shift gears and let go. The reason some people don't possess brilliant resilience is because they hold onto things long after others have moved on.

- *Brilliant Resilience* is recovering every ounce of hope that may have leaked out because of an issue or problem.

- *Brilliant Resilience* is uncovering hidden opportunities disguised as hard work.

- *Brilliant Resilience* is sticking your neck out to lead the pack instead of waiting for someone else to step up.

- *Brilliant Resilience* is putting one foot in front of the other toward what will work instead of what did work.

- *Brilliant Resilience* is creating your own mental stimulus plan and executing it every day.

Brilliant Resilience
is writing your vision
down, reading it daily,
repeating it in front of
the mirror, acting like
it is your truth, and
watching it unfold like
a lovely flower right
before your eyes.

HURRY@WORK
Self-Test

Do you identify with Hurry?

Score each statement below on a scale of 1 to 10. So, 1 is strongly disagree and 10 is strongly agree.

1. _____ Don't bother me with the details. I am a big-picture person. Let's get this project over with so I can get on to the next one.

2. _____ I have so much on my plate to do. I must hurry through this project or I will be further behind.

3. _____ My packed work schedule is stressing me out.

4. _____ I sense that the volume of work I quickly complete is diminishing the quality or excellence of it.

5. _____ I miss opportunities to add value in my work because I have too much on my plate.

6. _____ I rush through my daily work schedule and I don't have time to think creatively and be innovative.

7. _____ My family complains that I don't spend enough time with them. I am too busy even for days off or vacations.

8. _____ Time to think, meditate, relax, and develop personal hobbies and pursuits just doesn't exist for me.

9. _____ I am so busy now that I procrastinate and put off doing the groundwork that would expand my future career growth and grow my business.

10. _____ I find myself working harder and harder, faster and faster, but not any smarter.

TOTAL _____ *(Add up your total.)*

If you scored between 50 and 70, hurrying/rushing/busyness are hindering your job performance and affecting the quality of your work.

If you scored between 70 and 90, you are significantly missing future opportunities as you hurry right past them.

If you scored over 90, your hurrying will probably lead you to stress-related health problems and burnout.

WORRY@WORK
Self-Test

Do you identify with Worry?

Score each statement below on a scale of 1 to 10. So, 1 is strongly disagree and 10 is strongly agree.

1. _____ When I think about my future performance, I worry about under performing, failing, and/or falling short of goals or expectations.

2. _____ I am overly critical of my work.

3. _____ I fear low evaluation of my work by my colleagues, supervisors, managers, or boss.

4. _____ I lack confidence in my skills and abilities to get my work done satisfactorily.

5. _____ I am unhappy with my job description and worry that I am not a good fit for what is expected of me at work.

6. _____ I doubt my ability to finish my work on time.

7. _____ When I dream about my future, my dreams are more like nightmares. I am pessimistic about my future.

8. _____ My worries and anxieties often cause me to feel depressed, discouraged, and defeated.

9. _____ I am unhappy with my work and worry about being demoted, put on probation, or even fired.

10. _____ I daydream or find myself distracted at work, which often causes me to procrastinate or fill my schedule with unproductive busyness.

TOTAL _____ *(Add up your total.)*

If you scored between 50 and 70, worry is hindering your job performance and causing you a lot of unhappiness at work.

If you scored between 70 and 90, you are significantly stymied at work and are unable to perform well or enjoy your work.

If you scored over 90, your worry will probably lead you to burnout, being continually stressed out, or quitting.

Endnotes

State of the Global Workplace: 2022 Report - Gallup

Angela Duckworth, author of *Grit*

Seth Godin, author of *The Practice*

Johnson O'Connor Research Foundation – Aptitude Testing and Research for College and Career Guidance (jocrf.org)

Thomas J. Wininger, author of *Your True DNA! – Discovering God's Gift Within You!*

Margaret Broadley, author of *Your Natural Gifts*

Dr. Jean Watson, author of *Caring Science as Sacred Science*

McKinsey, "What is Resilience," McKinsey Insights, Jan. 17, 2023

King James Version of The Bible

Christine King, LinkedIn article "People, Skills, and Transformation"

"6 Profound Lessons that Surfing Can Teach Us About Life," by Lac Campbell

San Diego Surfing School – Online article about finding balance

"What Surfing Teaches You About Life" – from Escape Haven

Chris Crowley and Henry Lodge, authors of *Younger Next Year*

Barbara Fredrickson, author, online article "Are You Getting Enough Positivity in Your Diet?" (berkeley.edu)

Recommended
READING LIST

Several books impacted me during my writing of Resilience@Work and I wanted to share a few with you.

Influence Is Your Superpower: The Science of Winning Hearts, Sparking Change, and Making Good Things Happen, by Zoe Chance

I first met Dr. Chance at an association event where she was the featured speaker. Needless to say, this Yale assistant professor was riveting to listen to. When you pick up her book it will not disappoint. My biggest takeaways were understanding deep listening and her "Life-Changing Magic of a Simple Frame." It's narrated by her, and if you love audio books, you will enjoy the warmth in her voice.

Win When They Say You Won't: Break Through Barriers and Keep Leveling Up Your Success, by Daphne E. Jones

I love this book for so many reasons. First of all, Daphne is brilliant! She has 30-plus years of experience in general management and senior executive-level roles at IBM, Johnson & Johnson, Hospira, and General Electric. Currently, she serves on three major Fortune 500 boards. This is the book that I wish I had read years ago when I was climbing the ladder at Disney. Her

EDIT (Envision, Design, Iterate, and Transform) methodology is a simple framework that can be applied to your personal or professional life.

The Adventures of a Real-Life Cable Guy, by Dan Armstrong

We were introduced at a mastermind event that was organized by our mutual friend – Kyle Wilson. This is an incredible story of honesty, hard work, and humility, along with lessons that you can apply wherever you are in life.

The Power of One More: The Ultimate Guide to Happiness and Success, by Ed Mylett

I listened to this book two times on my morning walks. I ordered copies for our entire family and told them that I would pay them to read it. This book is simple, with actionable takeaways. His insight into the movie *The Matrix* will shift your thinking in how you see yourself.

The Prepared Leader: Emerge From Any Crisis More Resilient Than Before, by Erika H. James & Lynn Perry Wooten

I love this book for so many reasons. First of all, Erika H. James is dean of the Wharton School of Business at the University of Pennsylvania and the first Black person to lead the business school. Lynn Perry Wooten is president of Simmons University, an institution with a rich tradition of empowering women-centered leaders and social-justice champions.

This book is a roadmap on how to be an effective leader in a hyper-connected world. It encapsulates more than two decades of the authors' research to convey how it has positioned them to navigate through the distinct challenges of today and tomorrow. Their insights have implications for every leader in every industry and every worker at every level.

Greenlights, by Matthew McConaughey

Get this book via Audible or Spotify. It's as if he pulls up a seat next to you with a bucket of warm buttery popcorn and tells you his life story. You will have an entire new respect for his depth, transparency, gut honesty, humor, and teachable moments.

Walt's Apprentice: Keeping the Disney Dream Alive,
by Dick Nunis

As a former cast member, I love this book for obvious reasons. There are many books written about Disney. This one really captures the mind of Walt from someone who worked directly for him. The wisdom, wit, and real-world applications are timely in light of Disney's continual evolution.

How to Change: The Science of Getting from Where You Are to Where You Want to Be, by Katy Milkman

I was writing a new book and my editor suggested that I read Katy's book. WOW... I am so glad that he did. The research is mind blowing. As a professor at The Wharton School of Business, she demystifies how to think about change through a fresh lens.

The Psychology of Winner: Ten Qualities of a Total Winner,
by Dr. Denis Waitley

This is a classic book by one of the fathers of the personal development/personal achievement movement. Dr. Waitley is almost 90 years of age, and when you sit with him, his mind is as sharp as a brand-new knife. This is one book that you will want to reference for the rest of your life.

You've Been Chosen: *Thriving Through the Unexpected,*
by Cynt Marshall

If you've watched *Shark Tank,* then you know that Mark Cuban is very selective about the investments he makes. Well, one of his best investments was hiring Cynt Marshall to be CEO of the Dallas Mavericks. She is the first Black female in the history of the National Basketball Association. She teaches powerful lessons on how to search for peace, avoid distractions, and what to do when life doesn't follow the plan.

Adrift: America in 100 Charts, by Scott Galloway

I have a confession to make. I binge listen to Pivot, a podcast that Scott cohosts with Kara Swisher. I do not agree with some of their worldviews, nevertheless I walk away with a better under-standing of domestic and global issues. Scott is a kind human being who is wicked smart, and reading this book is a must. The research is simple, straightforward, and staggering.

32 Ways to Be a Champion in Business, by Earvin "Magic" Johnson

This book is one of my favorites. Magic Johnson was a beast on the court. However, off the court, he has taken the game of business into a new stratosphere. Go inside the mind of a legend and understand how to win at life and business.

Atomic Habits: An Easy & Proven Way to Build Good Habits & Break Bad Ones, by James Clear

A friend suggested this book. I am so glad they did. I had to relisten to the first chapter three times. It was that rich and really invited me to think differently. I know you will enjoy it as well.

The Myth of Normal: Trauma, Illness, and Healing in a Toxic Culture, by Gabor Mate, MD, and Daniel Mate

My dear friend Dan Valha invited me to attend a Global Exchange Event where the opening speaker was Dr. Mate. I was blown away and had to get his book right away. This book has helped me understand some of the trauma in my past life. If you know anyone who wants to put the pieces of the puzzle of their life together, then I highly recommend this book.

Cash Uncomplicated: A New Mindset to Building Wealth, by Aaron Nannini

Aaron is the real deal. He teaches why you shouldn't compare yourself to the Joneses, because the Joneses might be broke. He breaks down so much in this book, which will simplify how you think about money in a fresh way.

What the 1% Know: How Everyday People Use Real Estate to Build Wealth, by Robert Sayre

Another friend of mine suggested this book and I read it in one setting. Powerful and actionable.

Blind Spot: The Global Rise of Unhappiness and How Leaders Missed It, by Jon Clifton, CEO of Gallup

In 2006, Gallup began conducting global research on subjective well-being (happiness). After 15 years of tracking, the number of people living their best lives has more than doubled, while the number of people living their worst lives has more than quadrupled. They state that leaders are not familiar with the growing divide between the haves and have-nots of a great life. This is called well-being inequality.

The Six Conversations: Pathways to Connecting in an Age of Isolation and Incivility, by Heather Holleman

I stumbled upon this book while listening to a podcast. Needless to say, I downloaded the book right away. The foreword is written by Gary Chapman (*The 5 Love Languages*) and this book has already influenced how I start conversations, listen during conversations, and gave me the best questions to ask during a conversation. Communication is everything, and this book will stretch you mentally, emotionally, and spiritually.

The Gap and The Gain: The High Achievers' Guide to Happiness, Confidence, and Success, by Dan Sullivan, with Dr. Benjamin Hardy

I had several friends tell me about this book. It's a game-changer. One of my biggest takeaways is how to train your brain to see GAINS and how to always measure backwards. I know a book is really good when I have to slow down and reread or relisten to what is resonating with me in that moment. That becomes the key takeaway from the book.

Leading with Kindness: How Good People Consistently Get Superior Results, by William F. Baker and Michael O'Malley

The editor for a new book that I am writing suggested that I pick up a copy of this book. I fell in love with the research and rigor that was applied to this virtuous topic, which can at best feel light and doesn't fit into business at all. One of the key sections is that kindness is not about likability. Nor is kindness weakness. This book identifies six ingredients of kindness – compassion, integrity, gratitude, authenticity, humility, and humor – none of which might readily spring to mind when envisioning the archetypal business leader.

Why We Sleep: Unlocking the Power of Sleep and Dreams, by Matthew Walker

One of my greatest challenges over the last few years is sleeping more than 4-5 hours per night. If you struggle with sleep, then I suggest this book. After understanding the science and importance behind sleep, I started averaging about 6 hours of sleep at least three nights per week. My goal is to graduate to 7 hours for at least four nights per week.

***White Fright: The Sexual Panic at the Heart of America's Racist
History,*** by Jane Dailey

First of all, please note that Jane is an associate professor
of American history in the history department and at the Law
School at the University of Chicago. Her undergrad degree is
from Yale University and she has a PhD from Princeton University. I stumbled upon this book while at Barnes & Noble. I was
stunned by her research and analysis.

Vibrate Higher Daily: Live Your Power, by Lalah Delia

This book is profound and powerful. She says, "We become
conduits by using our light, voice, and unique gifts to channel
empowering healing energies that counterbalance the ways the
world is being misled, wounded, emotionally triggered, torn
apart, and underserved." I have highlighted this book, dogged
pages, and continue to reference it. Thank you, Kyle Wilson, for
giving me this book as a gift. WOW…it truly spoke to the core
of my soul.

***Of Boys and Men: Why the Modern Male Is Struggling, Why It
Matters, and What to Do About It,*** by Richard V. Reeves

This book stopped me in my tracks. I downloaded it from
audible and have listened to it three times. Please do yourself a
favor and make this book a part of your book club right away. His
research is spot on and his recommendations are very timely. I've
heard about the crisis that is happening with men around the
world. After listening to this book, it clicked. As a father, son,
brother, cousin, and nephew, I will have to step up even more.

Ignite the Power of Women in Your Life: A Guide for Men

I know what you are thinking. Women don't need their power ignited. However, they do need men to respect them. Men, there are things I want you to know, and I took the liberty to say it for you. Women, there are things that men are dealing with silently that they don't say to you. So I decided to take one for the team and say what's uncomfortable and true. There's a six-week e-course based on a book for individuals and businesses.

Ok, that's all for now.

Other Resources

BrilliantU™

BrilliantU,™ powered by Simon T. Bailey International, is a personal development platform designed to help individuals unlock their full potential and achieve their goals. Whether you are looking to advance your career, improve your relationships, or enhance your personal well-being, BrilliantU™ has something to offer.

Brilliant COACHING™

With over 30 years of experience in enabling individuals, teams, and organizations to reach their maximum potential, our coaching program is designed to deliver tailored solutions that meet your unique needs. Our customized programs comprise Inspirational Leadership, Managerial Essentials, Executive Development, DEIB Leadership, and Personal Development. Our approach involves conducting business reviews, using pre- and post-KPIs, facilitating assessments, and delivering comprehensive impact reports. Whether you're an individual or an organization, we create a program that aligns with your specific goals and objectives.

LINKEDIN LEARNING COURSE

Growing Relationships as a Manager will show you how to take more interest in people and their work to develop mutual, shared workplace commitments. You will learn the value of providing focused attention, taking time away from the office or the plant to discuss ideas and opinions, making time for meaningful conversation, and being open and available to your team.

Meet
SIMON T. BAILEY

Hello, O' Brilliant One. My name is Simon T. Bailey and, along with my team, we purposefully aspire to spark brilliance within individuals to lead communities, companies, and countries differently.

Our foundation is built on my 35-year professional journey, including working as sales director of Disney Institute and five other hospitality companies. Over the past 20 years, our scrappy personal development practice has served 2,300 organizations within 54 countries. LinkedIn Learning hosts three of our courses that have reached 250,000 students in more than 100 countries.

Individuals committed to next-level living have experienced our 10 published books, a viral video with 91M+ views, a *Daily Spark Podcast, Spark You,* and a robust community—Brilliant U and an inspiring blog that seeks to hug people with words. Above all, my team and I love God and our families and look forward to serving you.

And that's exactly what resilience is.

Books + E-books
BY SIMON T. BAILEY

Scan the QR code to begin reading.

**To Purchase Bulk Copies
of *Resilience @ Work:***

hello@simontbailey.com | 407-970-1113

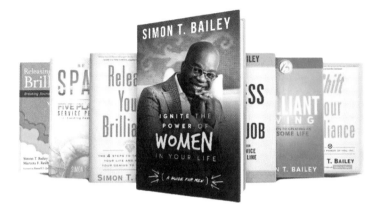

- ***Ignite the Power of Women in Your Life:*** *A Guide for Men*

- ***Be the Spark:*** *Five Platinum Service Principles for Creating Customers for Life*

- ***Success Is an Inside Job*** with bonus book ***Brilliant Service is the Bottom Line***

- ***Release Your Brilliance:*** *The 4 Steps to Transforming Your Life and Revealing Your Genius to the World* (also available in Spanish and Portuguese)

- ***Shift Your Brilliance:*** *Harness the Power of You, Inc.*

- ***Brilliant Living:*** *31 Insights to Creating an Awesome Life*

- ***Releasing Leadership Brilliance:*** *Breaking Sound Barriers in Education* co-written with Dr. Marceta F. Reilly

- ***Meditate on Your Personal Brilliance***

- ***Meditate on Your Professional Brilliance***

Connect
WITH SIMON T. BAILEY

Sign up for our free weekly newsletter and free digital gift:
www.simontbailey.com

Simon's blog:
www.simontbailey.com/blog/

Follow Simon:
https://www.instagram.com/simontbailey/

Listen to Simon:
https://www.youtube.com/c/SimonTBaileyIntl

Link with Simon:
www.linkedin.com/in/simontbailey

Book Simon to Speak at Your Event:
hello@simontbailey.com | 407-970-1113